Artistic Template

I0473039

Journey to...

SPACE
Volume 1

Artistic Template Journey to Space: Volume 1
Publisher: Basenji Studios LLC

Since we first looked to the heavens, humanity has been mesmerized by space and the stars. We have created shapes from the stars, created stories and tales from the shapes. In those stories we have sought comfort, understanding, and insight into the future. The secrets and mysteries of space have fueled technological advances and scientific insight for centuries. The relationship between humanity and the celestial sky is ever changing and limited only by the imagination.

Join us as we sketch the templates and, you, interstellar traveler, provide the artistic color on this Journey to...SPACE.

Artistic Templates assist all skill levels in honing their artistic skills and create true masterpieces. These are not mere coloring book pages but detailed scenes that allow your creativity to flourish. As you add life to the scene, the outlines recede, leaving only your creation to showoff and enjoy. The templates are designed to be used with any artistic medium so you can utilize your favorite brushes, paints, pastels, crayons, colored pencils, or other art supplies to see where your imagination takes you.

Artistic Templates work best if they are used on the paper that best corresponds to your chosen art medium. These designs are perfect for beginners trying to hone their skills or busy artists looking for a relaxing, yet challenging, experience.

Get printouts of the Templates, order other Templates on specialized paper, and get creative ideas at: artistictemplate.com

Discover more Artistic Templates at: artistictemplate.com, Amazon, and other e-retailers.

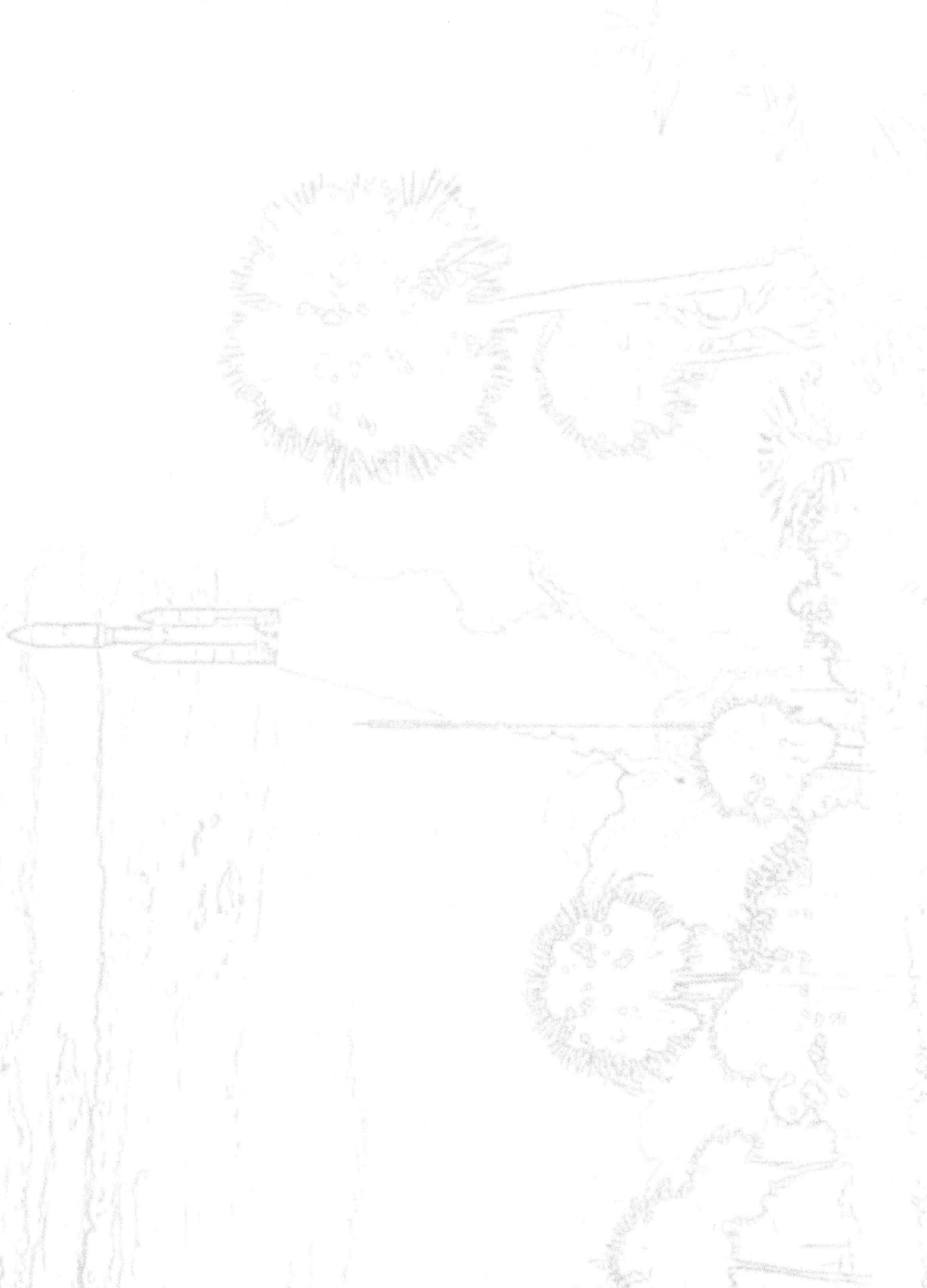

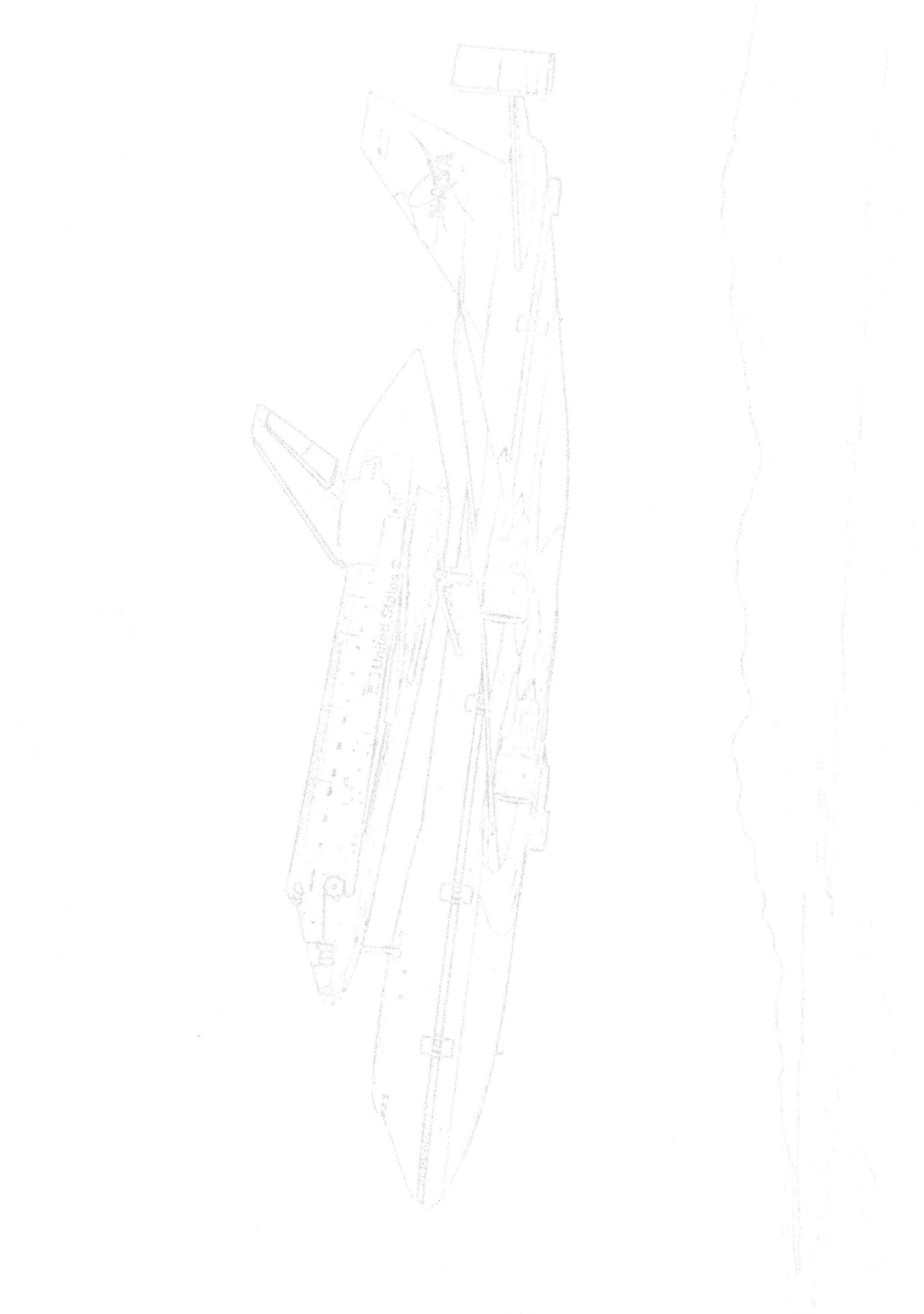

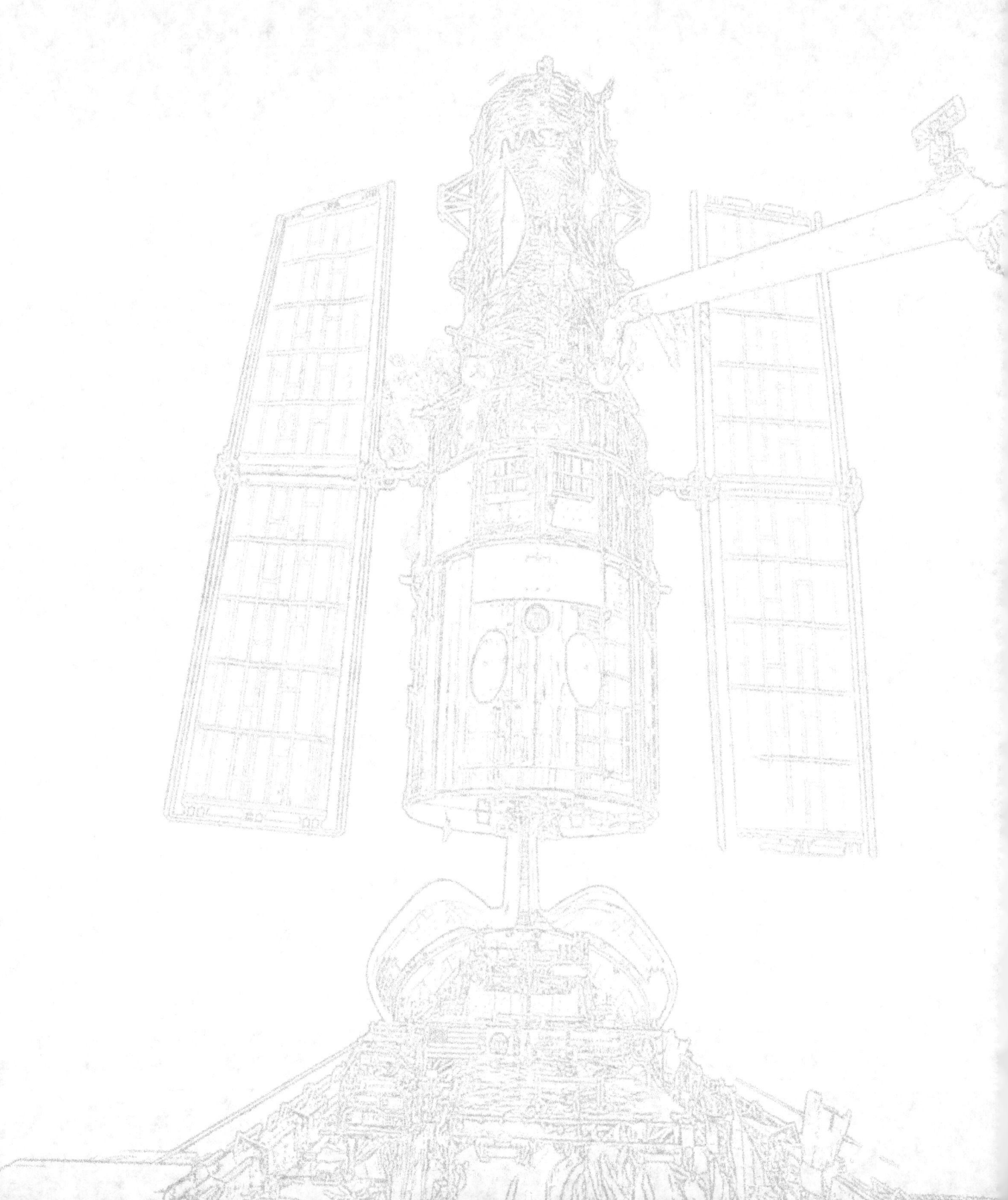

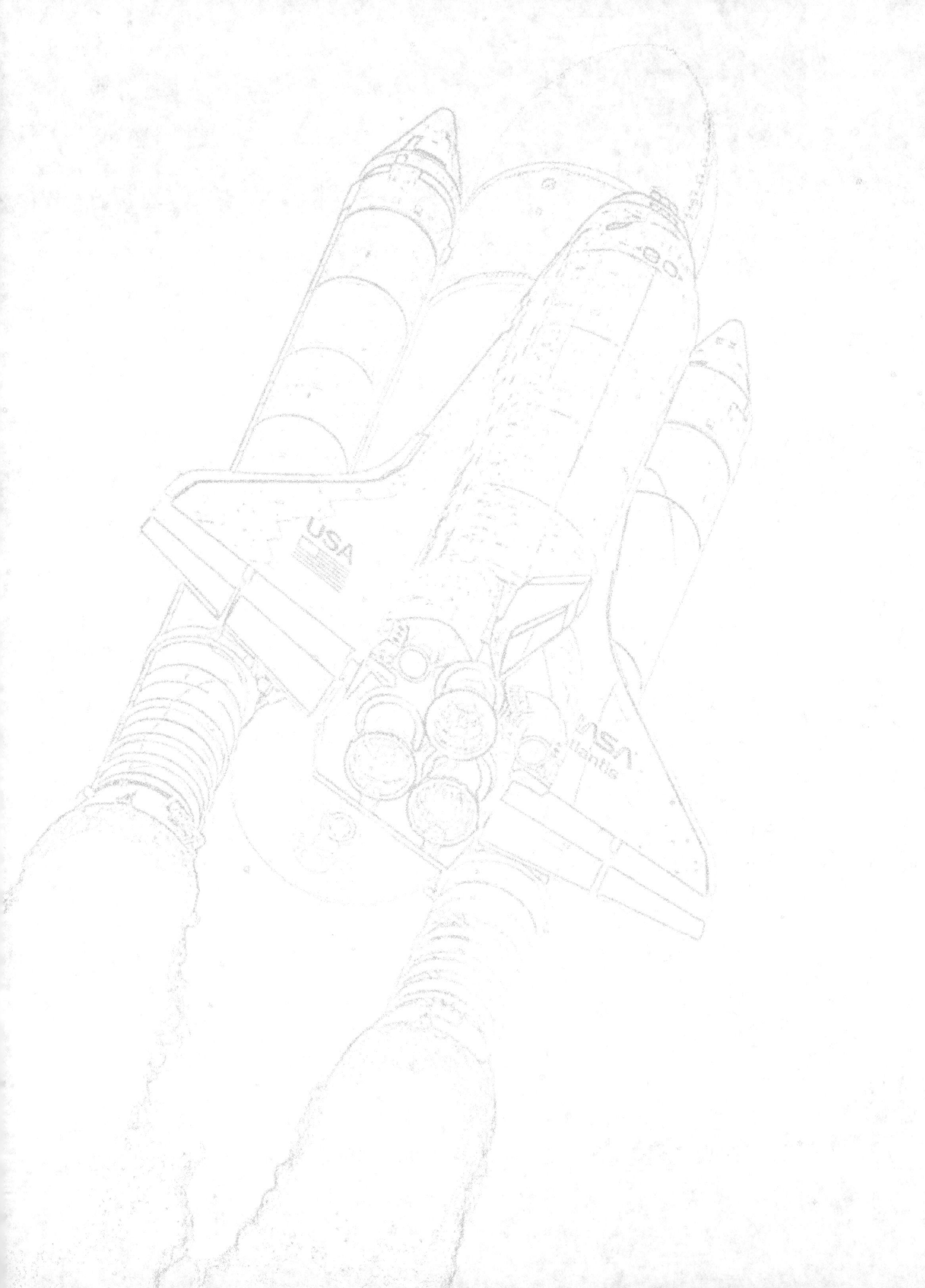

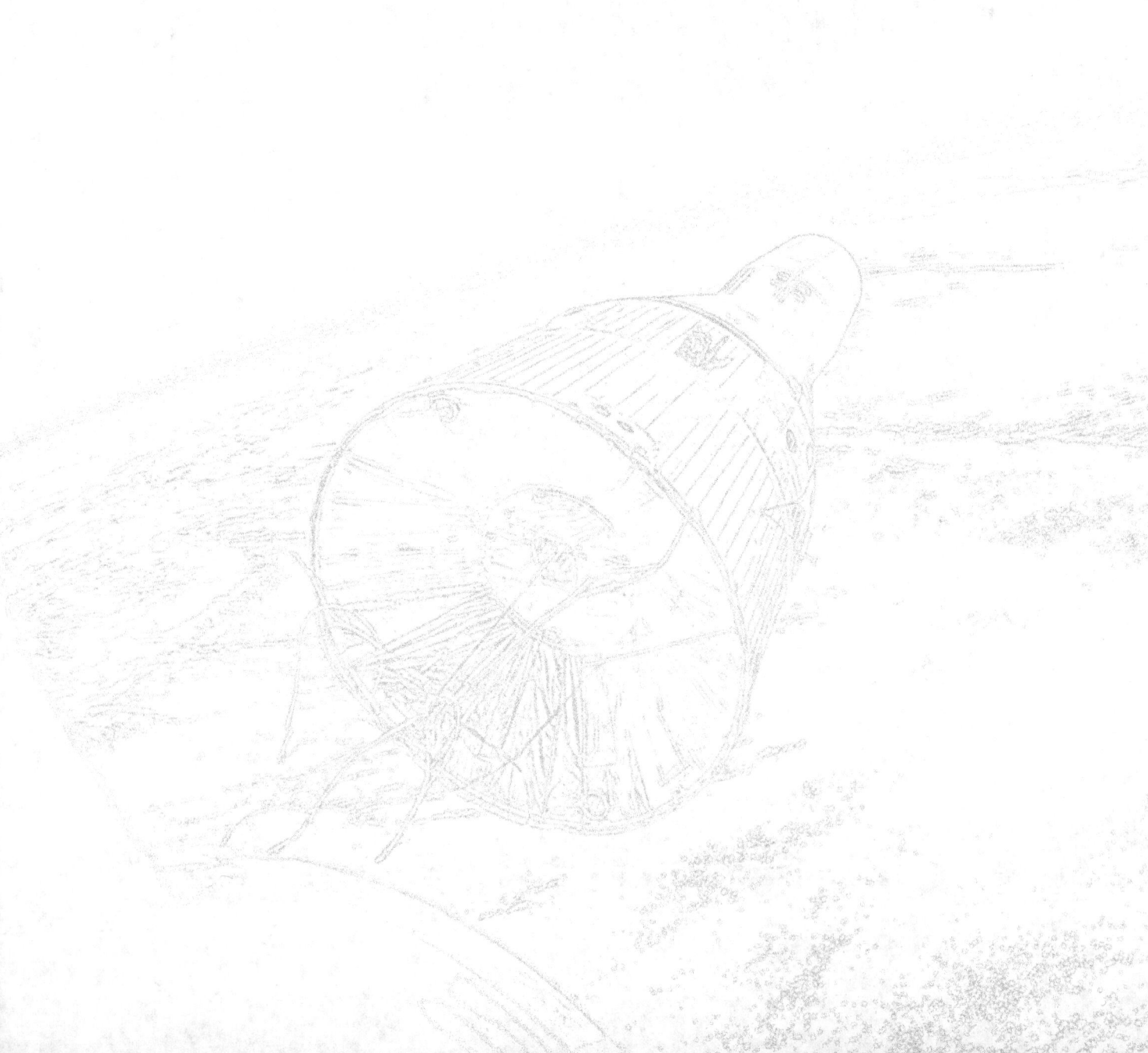

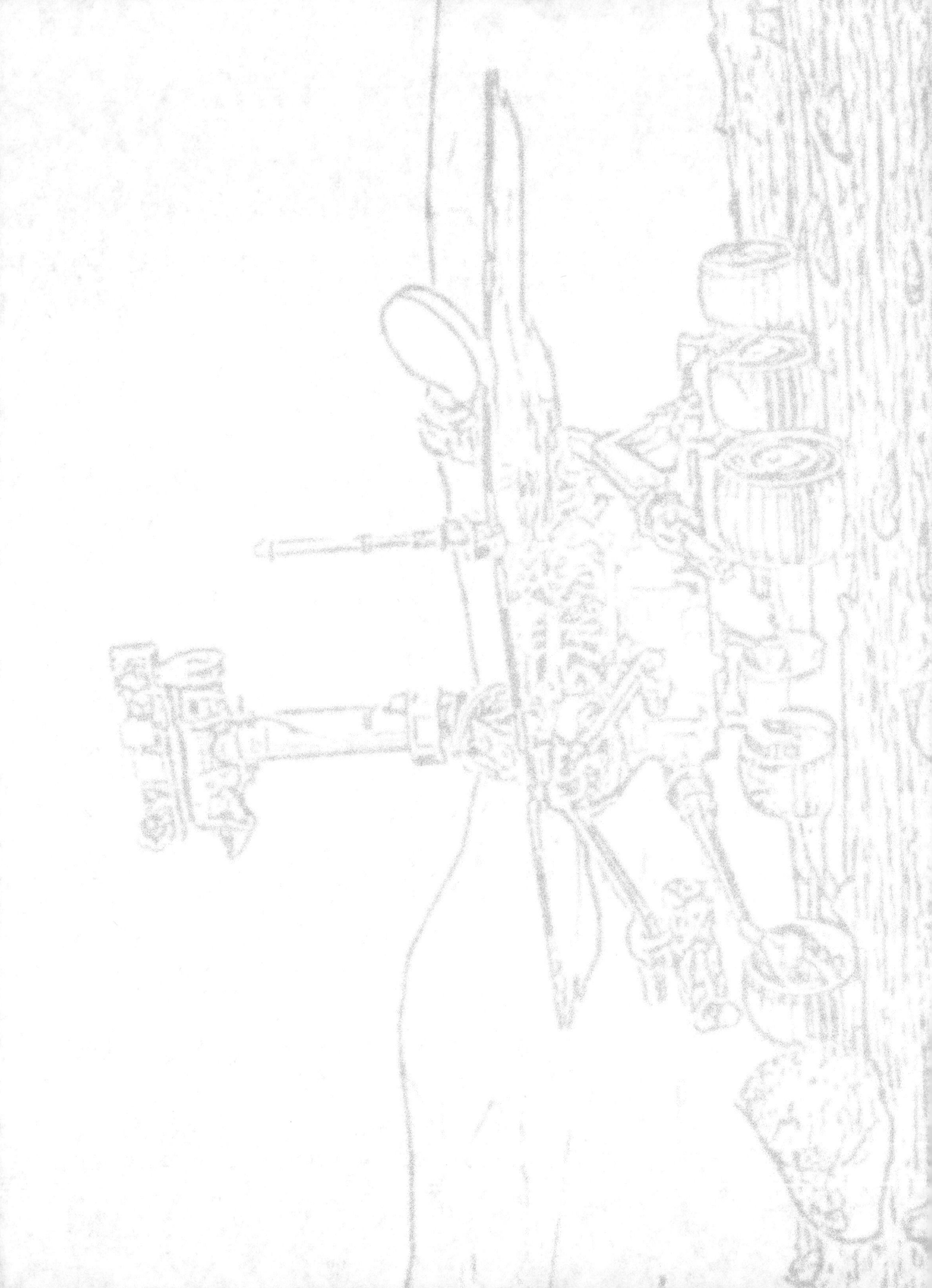

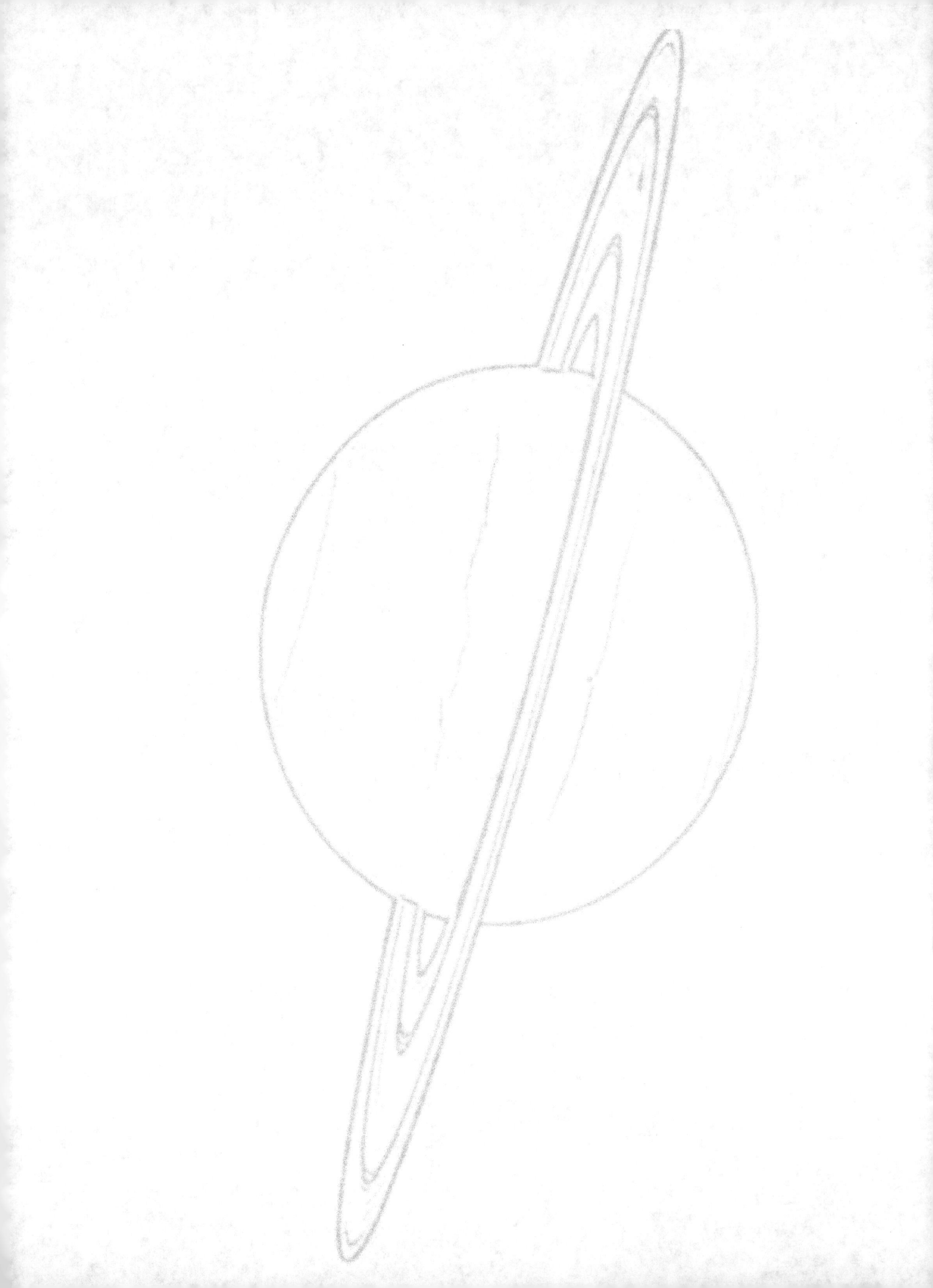

We hoped you enjoyed your time in space.

Please visit our website www.artistictemplate.com for new and different adventures.

If you have any feedback please email us at staff@basenjistudio.com and please leave us a review!

Thank you and enjoy your art!

www.ingramcontent.com/pod-product-compliance
Lightning Source LLC
Chambersburg PA
CBHW081025170526
45158CB00010B/3159